THE CENTER FOR DOCUMENTARY PHOTOGRAPHY

The Center for Documentary Photography, established in 1980 by Duke University's Institute of Policy Sciences and Public Affairs, grew out of the institute's long-term interest in photography and, more broadly, in the relation between the humanities and public policy.

The educational programs of the center include undergraduate courses, exhibitions and lectures by visiting photographers, and opportunities for independent field work by outstanding students. The center will publish several books, of which this is the first, and has begun a photographic archive at the Duke library, chiefly of works relating to the South. The activities of the center are being supported by the Lyndhurst Foundation of Chattanooga, Tennessee.

In making a serious commitment to documentary photography in the university, we have hoped to show the value of visual language in a highly verbal place. Through study of the documentary tradition and through the use of the camera, students are encouraged to see more deeply into facts and ideas. Education is more than the accumulation of knowledge. It is, or ought to be, the development of sensibility, of capacities for discernment and reflection, of a readiness to act on what is believed.

For those who care about the shape and direction of modern American life, documentary photography has much to offer. Taking photographs seriously is one way of encouraging and altering the pictures we carry with us in our minds. Paul Kwilecki's pictures, like those of other gifted photographers, can make us pause and wonder, and recognize how much richer and more complicated the world is than any of the things we say about it.

This book exists principally because of the extraordinary generosity of the Lyndhurst Foundation, the encouragement of Robert Coles, and the help of Rich Hendel and Iris Hill at the University of North Carolina Press. Our gratitude to them and to others who have helped is great.

BRUCE L. PAYNE
Lecturer in Policy Sciences and Public Affairs
Duke University

Understandings

Photographs of Decatur County, Georgia
by Paul Kwilecki

Introduction by Alex Harris

Published for The Center for Documentary Photography

by The University of North Carolina Press Chapel Hill

Manufactured in the United States of America

Library of Congress Cataloging in Publication Data
Kwilecki, Paul, 1928–
Understandings : Photographs of Decatur
County, Georgia.

1. Decatur County (Ga.)—Description and travel—
Views. 2. Decatur County (Ga.)—Social life and
customs—Pictorial works. I. Duke University.
Center for Documentary Photography. II. Title.
F292.D27K85 975.8′993043 81-2958
ISBN 0-8078-1486-5 AACR2

FOR CHARLOTTE

Deep in southwest Georgia, on a stretch of land thirty-three miles long and thirty-two miles wide, Paul Kwilecki has photographed for the last twenty years.

Kwilecki was born in Bainbridge, Georgia, the county seat of Decatur County in 1928, and with the exception of five years at Emory University in Atlanta, he has not left the county for any length of time. For most of his adult life, he owned and ran a large hardware store, I. Kwilecki's Sons Inc., which served the primarily agricultural county. Kwilecki's grandfather and father were also prominent merchants and civic leaders in Bainbridge. In 1952, he married Charlotte Williford, a musician and piano teacher from nearby Camilla, Georgia, and they raised their four children within a few miles of the house where Kwilecki himself was brought up.

Around 1956, in a photographic magazine, Kwilecki came across a series of Eugene Smith's photographs of a Spanish village. These images changed his life. He purchased a 35-mm camera and began to photograph around Bainbridge. By 1960 he was determined to make a photographic record of Decatur County as he, a native, saw it. Photography became his passion. He would leave the store to photograph at odd hours, whenever he could spare some time, returning to wait impatiently until closing so that he could develop and print his film.

Although Kwilecki has worked in a remote place, away from museums, exhibitions, or other photographers with whom he might discuss his project, he was never a naive artist, even in his early work. He started his own photographic library, and was impressed by the photographs of Sander, Atget, Hine, Curtis, Gilpin, and particularly the warm, intimate work of Eugene Smith. Kwilecki began a long correspondence with David Vestal, a noted photographer and teacher. Those letters sustained him through what he has called "my years in isolation and solitude."

Paul Kwilecki has chosen to photograph his home, one small county in the South where he is known and trusted. The photographs are his reaction and response to Decatur County. His is a particular vision, different in important ways from those that preceded it.

Our modern view of the South has been shaped largely by photographers with other purposes or working methods than those of Kwilecki, by men and women sent on assignment in the South to depict towns and counties often unfamiliar to them. Some of the best-known photographs from the 1930s and early 1940s were made in this way by Farm Security Administration photographers like Walker Evans, Dorothea Lange, and Arthur Rothstein, who traveled through the South with their cameras.

Roy Stryker, the director of the photographic division of the FSA, wanted his photographers to show the depth of distress in part of the country to those Americans who had not experienced the depression. Most of the photographers shared this common mission. They looked with compassion on the hard lives of the Americans they portrayed. The result in the majority of photographs was not only an image, but a message.

The South they revealed was, at worst, seriously depressed in economy and spirit. At best, its people were typically portrayed as hardworking, usually serious individuals, whose stoicism in the face of tremendous social and economic difficulties conferred on them a hard-won dignity.

The FSA photographs are a valuable part of the cumulative visual history of this country. But there is also much to learn from the photographs Eudora Welty made during the same period in her native Mississippi. Her vision of the South is a more intimate one, full of images that show the joy of living, even at the depth of the depression. Welty was a part of the society she photographed. She was not on assignment or out to prove anything with her camera. Grouped together, Welty's pictures have the quality of a large family album and show dimensions of life not captured in much of the work of the FSA photographers.

Thirty years before the Great Depression, there was a real distinction between the artistic and the documentary approach in American photography. There were those, like Alfred Stieglitz, for whom the medium and the beauty of the image were all important. Stieglitz's life work was dedicated to proving that photography was an art in its own right. For others, like Jacob Riis, the subject was all that mattered. Riis photographed to expose conditions in New York City's slums at the turn of the century. For Riis, photography was visual proof of a social condition, not an end in itself. He was not concerned with beautiful pictures, nor with composition and form.

By the 1930s the differences between documentary and art photography were no longer clear. Many photographers consciously fused form and content in their work. Among those who helped to blur these distinctions were Walker Evans, one of the principal FSA photographers, and Lewis Hine, an independent documentary photographer who exposed working conditions for children in early industrial America. In Evans's photographs it was overwhelmingly evident that one could create both an aesthetic object as well as a powerful remark on something seen. Lewis Hine certainly understood that for his work to have the maximum social impact, the photographs needed to be beautiful, in and of themselves.

By the time Paul Kwilecki began to photograph in Decatur County, it was no longer assumed that photography was a highly objective medium. The documentary tradition he inherited left much room for the interpretation of the photographer. Kwilecki has chosen to draw on that tradition very broadly. He has wanted to record as well as to reflect on the diversity of life in the county. He has an eye for beauty, but also sees the accumulating ironies of his time and place. Like any accomplished artist, Kwilecki has been influenced by the work that has come before him. But a greater influence has been Decatur County. Kwilecki's life in the county has formed his views, his reactions, and the way he sees. His photographs are firmly rooted to that place.

Paul Kwilecki's work in photography reflects his qualities as a man. He has great doubts and real passion. He combines a strong character with genuine modesty— a rare accomplishment. It is in his nature to be truthful, to show exactly how he feels about things. Kwilecki is a fine and careful craftsman, yet his pictures show no trace of pretentiousness. The mannerisms of misapplied technique simply do not appear in his work. In each of his photographs, there is a maturity of vision and an understanding that is uniquely his own. Over the years, Kwilecki has worked in a way that has gone against much of what has proven popular in photography.

Currently, photographs that shock the viewer because of their exotic content or highly personal style are much appreciated. For photographers working in this vein, a definite point of view often emerges from the search for personal style. Their photographs tell us that all life can be seen in a certain way. Kwilecki's photographs are more complex. While he has his own concise way of seeing, there is no general or preconceived point of view. There are no absolutes of tone or style.

Over the years, Paul Kwilecki has worked by photographing one part of Decatur County at a time, usually for six months to a year. He has then chosen ten or fifteen prints depicting that particular subject and organized them into a series. Only then has he moved on to the next thing. In twenty years, Kwilecki's photographs of Decatur County have grown into a sizable body of work, containing series on the Flint River, Willis Park, the Decatur County Courthouse, the Trailways bus station, churches, cemeteries, residences, professions, the downtown area, carnivals and special days, shade tobacco workers, a group he entitled "Icons—Sacred and Profane," and many others.

But there are some series we do not see in the body of Kwilecki's work, some he has simply never made. Kwilecki has photographed what interested him. He has not conducted a survey or dissected every aspect of life in Decatur County. A social scientist might find "significant" gaps in what is portrayed. For instance, Kwilecki does not emphasize the wealthy people of the county, although there are undoubtedly wealthy people living there. More often than not, he has aimed his camera at the poor or middle class blacks and whites of the county. He has photographed the sort of people about whom Flannery O'Connor has written, "the mystery of existence is always showing through the texture of their ordinary lives."*

With the exception of the last sections of this book, Kwilecki presents his photographs here out of series, as individual or paired images. His method of working has been to photograph one subject at a time. This is not necessarily the way the photographs must be seen. An appreciation of Kwilecki's photographs comes from more than the knowledge of how they were made, or what particular activity or aspect of county life they show. We respond to these images not only for the information in them or for their social implications, but for aesthetic and emotional reasons as well.

Kwilecki's portrayal of Decatur County goes beyond an affectionate portrait by a native son. His photographs comment on the beauty of Decatur County, but also

*From *Mystery and Manners*.

make a strong statement about the tawdry nature of the place. As in any close and lasting relationship, there are negative feelings that struggle with the more positive and loving ones. Life in Decatur County has both nourished and wounded the photographer. His eye can be critical and stinging. But again and again, one finds in his pictures a marvelous and affectionate sense of humor.

This is important and courageous work on many levels. Kwilecki has stepped away from the everydayness of his own life, while scrutinizing that life very closely. He has spent over twenty years taking a deep look at both his community and himself. He has risked being misunderstood at home and elsewhere: at home for appearing more than a little eccentric in his wanderings with the camera, and outside of Decatur County for seeming a small-town or strictly regional photographer. The best southern writers have always known that by looking into the vernacular one can find the country as a whole. Kwilecki must know this as well.

Paul Kwilecki is extremely serious in his commitment to his photographic project. In 1975 he sold his hardware business in order to devote full time to photography, a career for which he had no guarantees of success. His work is ongoing. He photographs and prints every day, scarcely pausing for the time necessary to help organize

this book. Several of the photographs that appear on these pages were made literally days before the final selection deadline. Kwilecki has recently received permission to photograph in a local hospital and in the County Courthouse while court is in session. These and a closer look at the landscape of the county will be his next project.

There is a strong mystical element involved in the making of any art. The best photographs spring from a part of the photographer he cannot know. They come out of the raw emotion that inhabits the unconscious mind. These photographs are unexpected, even for the one who has made them.

In a letter to me in 1975, Paul Kwilecki wrote, "How it is here, how it looks, feels, tastes, smells, at this particular instant in time, and to this particular human being, that's what I'm after." Kwilecki's photographs are about ordinary people in a very ordinary place. But their meaning goes beyond that, beyond what the photographer has consciously set out to do. The people he photographs appear both real and archetypal. In preserving something of the lives of the people of Decatur County, he helps us preserve something of our humanity as well.

ALEX HARRIS
Director, Center for
Documentary Photography
Duke University

ACKNOWLEDGMENTS

Many people had a part in the seeing that led to these photographs by shaping the feeling and point of view from which the seeing came.

I wish to acknowledge the debt I owe the people of Decatur County. They have nurtured me mostly on openness and trust. The affection I have for them, the honor I would do them, constitutes the affirmative part of this work. Equally important, the negative, satirical parts are my response to the wounds they have inflicted on themselves as well as on me, without knowing or meaning to.

My thanks to David Vestal. Although not my teacher in the strictest sense, he is the most important teacher I ever encountered. He renewed my belief in the art of stimulating a student to learn. In 1961 I wrote him to ask if he would look at some of my prints and give me his opinion of them. He wrote back saying that he would give me his honest reaction, which might not be kind but was the only thing that could do me any good. An interchange of prints and letters followed that lasted about ten years. From this exchange I obtained advice, taste, and encouragement, but most of all a bracing energy and thrust that kept my spirit alive. David himself has little comprehension of what I owe him.

Alex Harris is another whose kindness and generosity I can never repay. If it were not for him, this book, quite literally, would not exist. It was completely his idea to publish my work as a book, and he has spent many more hours getting it into shape than I. Only another photographer can appreciate the joy of working with a publisher who loves the work and takes it as seriously as its author. Thank you, Alex.

I would also like to thank the National Endowment for the Arts, which gave me a major grant for the year 1980. The money was useful, but of more importance was the endorsement of an official body whose amen to my project assured me that my work was of interest outside Decatur County.

Finally, and most important of all, thanks to my wife, Charlotte. This body of work has, from our point of view, been painful and long in coming. Much of it originates in my dissatisfaction, frustration, and rage. Without her belief once faltering, she patiently waited for me to work through all of it, emerging on the other side with something affirmative and, we believe, original, something we can both take pride in. In every sense it is her book as much as mine.

Men are admitted into Heaven not because they have
curbed & govern'd their Passions or have No Passions,
but because they have Cultivated Their Understandings.
The Treasures of Heaven are not Negations of Passion,
but Realities of Intellect, from which all the Passions Emanate
Uncurbed in their Eternal Glory.
The Fool shall not enter into Heaven let him be ever so Holy.
Holiness is not the Price of Entrance into Heaven.
Those who are cast out are All Those who, having no Passions
of their own because No Intellect, Have spent their lives in
Curbing & Governing other people's by the Various
arts of Poverty & Cruelty of all kinds.

From William Blake's "A Vision of the Last Judgement"

21

35

Decatur County Courthouse

Churches and Cemeteries

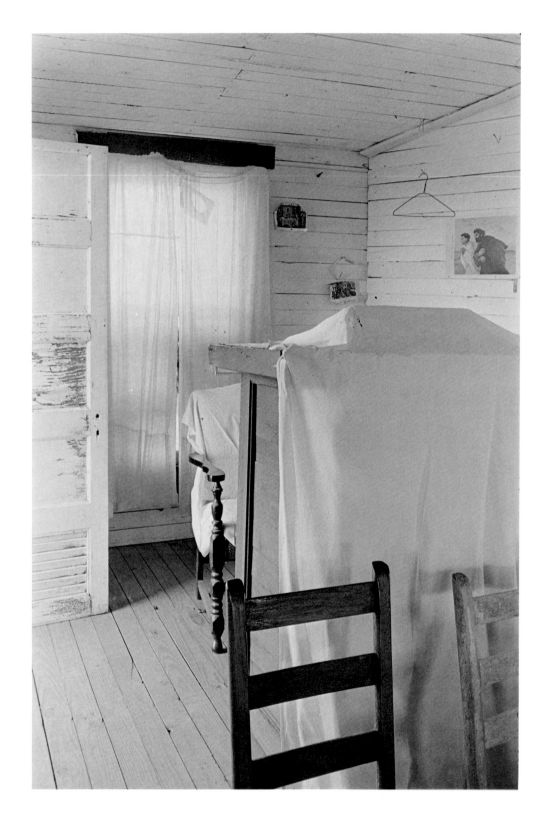

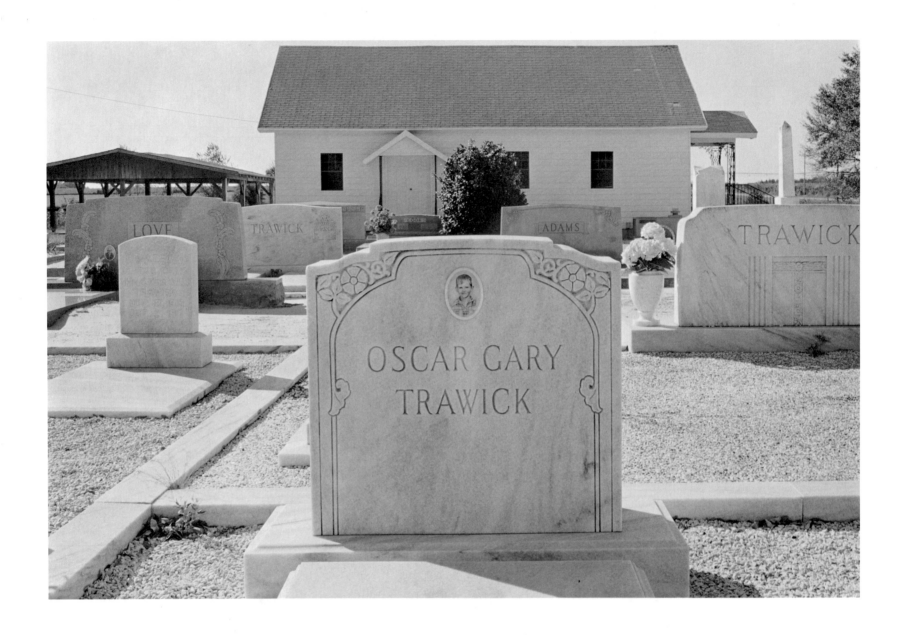

Baptism

These photographs were taken in the city of Bainbridge or in other areas of Decatur County, Georgia. The name of the photographic series is given in parentheses.

Frontispiece: Oak City Cemetery, 1974 (Cemetery)